Giant
Cave Crocs!

Rob Waring, *Series Editor*

NATIONAL GEOGRAPHIC
LEARNING

Australia · Brazil · Mexico · Singapore · United Kingdom · United States

Words to Know

This story is set in Africa, in the country of Madagascar [mæedəgæskər]. It takes place in a place called Ankarana [æenkæerənə] in the northern part of the country.

 Crocs! Read the definitions. Then complete the paragraph with the correct form of the words.

amphibious: able to live both on land and in water
cave: a hole in the ground, usually with an opening in the side of a hill or mountain
herpetologist: a scientist who studies cold-blooded creatures
reptile: an animal that lays eggs and has cold blood, such as a snake
species: a specific group of living things that have similar characteristics

Crocodiles—or 'crocs' for short—are large (1)_____. All crocodiles are (2)_____ so they can live on land and in water. Most live above the ground along rivers or lakes, but there have been reports of an unusual (3)_____ of crocodile that lives in Madagascar. This type of crocodile may have left the outdoor rivers and moved deep under the earth to live in (4)_____. Two scientists, a biologist and a (5)_____, are going to follow the footprints of these huge animals to find out if they really exist!

crocodile

2

B Studying Crocodiles. Read the paragraph. Then complete the definitions with the correct form of the underlined words and phrases.

Crocodiles have been around so long that they are sometimes referred to as 'living dinosaurs.' Not much is known, however, about the cave crocs of Madagascar, so an expedition is going there to research them. A team of scientists plans to capture a cave crocodile and take a small tissue sample from the animal's body. Then, a geneticist can study the tissue in order to see how cave crocs are related to other crocs of the world.

1. _____ is a scientific term for a small piece of an animal or person.

2. An _____ is a journey organized for a special purpose.

3. _____ means to catch or to take by force.

4. _____ are huge animals that lived on Earth a long time ago, but which no longer exist.

5. A _____ is a scientist who studies the passing of physical characteristics from generation to generation.

cave

footprint

Crocodiles are large reptiles that have been living on Earth for millions of years. Because they have been around for so long, they have sometimes been called 'living dinosaurs.' These amphibious animals make both land and water their home. But now, scientists believe that crocodiles may live somewhere else—deep beneath the earth in Madagascar!

Madagascar is one of the most remarkable places on Earth. This very large island broke away from the rest of the continent of Africa during the age of the dinosaurs. The caves where these rare crocodiles are supposed to live are located in Ankarana, a distant region in northern Madagascar. These unusual animals only exist in an area that isn't very easy to get to, and tracking them down is considerably difficult.

🎧 CD 1, Track 03

Skim for Gist

Read through the entire book quickly to answer the questions.

1. What is the reader basically about?

2. What are some things that the scientists experience in the story?

So, there are really crocodiles in the caves of Ankarana, aren't there? Nobody is sure, so Dr. Brady Barr, an American herpetologist, has traveled all the way to Madagascar to find out. Dr. Barr is one of the world's leading experts on crocodiles, but this is his first expedition to the African island. He's come to discover whether or not these very rare cave crocodiles really exist. Gerardo Garcia, a biologist from Spain, will be joining Dr. Barr to look through the caves in which the crocodiles supposedly live.

Very little is known about cave crocodiles and why they may have chosen to live underground. However, in this region, **poachers**[1] are always trying to kill crocodiles. The caves of Ankarana may have become the last safe place to which they can escape. Another possible reason that these crocodiles may have moved into caves is that they are somehow different. Are these cave crocs the same species that is found elsewhere in Madagascar? That's a question that no one can really answer right now. Scientists have never actually captured one of the crocs deep in the cave. But perhaps that's about to change …

[1] **poacher:** a person who hunts animals illegally

After a long journey by helicopter, Dr. Barr joins Garcia to make the boat trip to the caves. As they row along the river, the two scientists remain quiet so they don't scare the crocs away. Finally, they reach one of the huge caves in which the crocodiles are said to live. Once they are inside, Dr. Barr talks with Garcia and their guide about the cave in which the crocodiles have been sighted, or seen. "So this is the 'Crocodile Cave,'" confirms Barr as he looks around, "This is where we're at." He then adds, "And it's **aptly**[2] named because this is where crocodiles have been sighted inside the cavern."

The local guide shows the two explorers a map of where the team will be going. The map indicates that they must make a difficult, all-day journey that will take them to the other side of a high **cliff**.[3] The group starts their underground expedition by walking into the mouth of the dark, wet cave. With a little luck, the group will see crocodiles in the cave, and hopefully catch them too!

----

[2]**aptly:** appropriately; correctly
[3]**cliff:** a high rock formation with a steep drop

As the scientists go deep into the cave system, they are guided only by the light of their **flashlights**.[4] No light can get this far underground. There are at least 98 kilometers* of caves inside the system. The cave system is one of Africa's largest, and it was formed millions of years ago.

As the group walks along, they must pay close attention to walk safely through the underground rivers that flow through the cave. But the team must also pay attention to something else: they must think about the goals of the expedition. Crocodiles don't usually live underground. So, are there really crocodiles in these caves? And if so, why are they there? Do they live here all year? These are the questions the expedition hopes to answer.

---

[4]**flashlight:** a small light (often hand-held) operated by batteries
*See page 32 for a metric conversion chart.

As the group finds their way through the dark, narrow **passageways**[5] and high open areas, Dr. Barr wonders at the size of the cave itself. "This is just huge. I mean it's, you know, a hundred feet high," he says, but then the sound of his voice suddenly changes. "Look over here," he says excitedly. The group quickly moves over to the area where Barr is shining his flashlight. "There's a big crocodile track right there, see? See that? Look at that!" he says with surprise. He then walks along the path of the tracks and explains to them, "There's a back footprint," he reports. "You see, it was going this direction," he says as he leads the group through the darkness. Suddenly, his light swings to the right, "Oh!" he says with even more excitement than before, "That's another one!"

The team is now on the path of not one, but two huge cave crocodiles! "I mean, these are big crocodiles," says Dr. Barr as he follows the footprints, "Look at that foot!" Barr then reaches down and touches one of the prints. He notices that it has not been long since the crocodile was there. "This looks very fresh," he comments. He holds his hand next to the mark left by the croc's foot— the footprint is actually bigger than his hand! "That's a big croc!" he says as he looks at the footprint and then ahead into the darkness. The group can't see much in the black cave, but Barr can tell where the animals are going by the footprints. "They're all going this way," he says and starts to move in that direction. As he does, he repeats once more in amazement: "These are big crocs!" It's hard to believe that Dr. Barr and the others may be only a few steps behind huge crocodiles—and it's happening deep under the ground!

[5]**passageway:** a walkway

After hours of difficult walking through the cave, the team finally exits into daylight once again. Then suddenly: "Whoa, whoa, whoa!" shouts Barr as he signals for the others to stop. "Look! Right here! Look at this!" he exclaims as he points to the ground. It's another set of footprints! "Look at that! That is a big croc!" says Barr with excitement. He looks carefully at the footprints and explains which ones they are, "Back left foot, right here. There's a right. That's a front right there." He then looks up and points, "It's going [in] this direction." He stops and looks at one of the tracks again, "Look at this. Man, that's **enormous!**"[6] he says in surprise. The team decides to measure the footprint; it's about 13 inches long. That means that this particular crocodile is about the size of a car!

---

[6]**enormous:** very large; huge

The team continues and sees signs of crocodiles everywhere, including more footprints and marks from their long tails. The group stops again, and Dr. Barr points to the ground. He explains that the front feet of crocodiles have five toes and the back feet have only four. He then shows the others the footprints. "Five. One, two, three, four, five," he says as he counts the front toe marks on a track. "There's a back," he then says as he points to a back foot marking, and counts the toes in order to show the team, "One, two, three ... only four."

The group follows the croc tracks through the dark caves. As they walk, they move their flashlights from side to side in hopes of seeing one of the mysterious crocs. Then, finally, they see something—eyes shining in the darkness. "Whoa! We've got an eye shine!" says Barr with excitement. His flashlight has hit the eyes of a crocodile and the light has been reflected back. This creates what he calls an 'eye shine.' "Look, look, look—croc!" cries Dr. Barr, excitedly. "Wait, wait, there's a croc!" he says to the team as he points across the cave, "Shh ... Look, see him? Eye shine ... right there, see it?" he says as the other men search for the eye shine. "It's moving! Let's go, it's going around the corner," he says, and the team goes after their first croc.

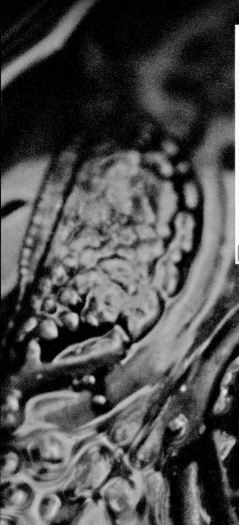

Fact Check: True or false?

1. The scientists have found very few crocodile footprints.

2. A crocodile's back foot has more toes than the front foot.

3. An 'eye shine' is light reflecting off eyes in the dark.

4. The team saw the crocodile first and then followed his tracks.

The men follow the crocodile around the corner of the cave. Suddenly, they realize that the croc has slipped into one of the underground rivers that run through the cave. Luckily, they're able to find the croc in the water; however, it's not the enormous crocodile they've been following. It's a much smaller, younger crocodile. That's not a problem for Barr, though. For him, all that matters is having a chance to examine one of these rare animals. If they can catch it, the little croc will be the first crocodile ever captured by scientists in this cave.

The scientists move carefully closer and closer to the croc, which is lying quietly near a large rock. Dr. Barr leans out over the water and reaches towards the croc. He slowly moves his hand closer and closer. The team is very quiet because they know that if Barr makes one wrong move, he could be bitten! Finally, Barr gets close enough and catches the little croc in one quick movement—and he does it using only his **bare**[7] hand!

---

[7] **bare:** uncovered and unprotected

Dr. Barr is very pleased: "Got it!" he says as he holds up the young crocodile proudly. "We've got a **Nile crocodile**[8] in a cave!" he says and laughs at the thought of it. "We [have] got a crocodile in a cave!" he repeats as if he can't believe it, "Look at that!" Suddenly the small crocodile starts making a strange sound. Dr. Barr explains, "That's the **distress**[9] cry. It's calling for its mom." He then pauses to look around the dark cave and comments, "There may be … some really big crocs in here."

He then turns his attention back to the young crocodile and adds, "And this croc is so small! It wouldn't surprise me if they were **nesting**[10] in here." Dr. Barr then hands the croc over to Garcia so he can take a small piece of tissue from its body for geneticists to study. With this tissue sample, they may be able to solve many of the mysteries about these crocodiles.

Barr then takes the time to show the others that crocodiles have extremely small sense organs all over their bodies. These sense organs feel very slight movements in the water and allow crocodiles to sense when a fish or an animal is near. Crocodiles don't need to see, hear, or even smell their food. They can 'feel' it, and then move quickly to catch and eat it. This makes crocodiles the perfect animal for hunting in complete darkness.

---

[8]**Nile crocodile:** one of the crocodile species found in Africa
[9]**distress:** emotional pain or suffering
[10]**nest:** create a home or area in which to raise young

After they finish taking the tissue sample and examining the croc, the team releases the animal back into the water. As the little croc quickly swims away, Dr. Barr comments to his team members, "That was great! Okay, let's go get mama! We've got to get a bigger one!" They continue their exploration of the dark, wet pathways to see if they can find more cave crocs. As they move deeper into the cave, they find themselves walking through knee-deep water. Not a pleasant thing to do with so many crocs around!

At last, the men find another croc, but this one is much bigger and in a difficult location. It's in a smaller, darker cave with a low ceiling. Dr. Barr must use his **capture pole**[11] to catch it. Barr has to walk through several feet of water to get to the animal. As he does this, the water gets deeper and deeper. Soon he's chest-deep in water in a very small space—and with a real live crocodile!

Brady remains calm as he carefully slips the rope from the capture pole around the croc's tail. He and the others then quickly pull the rope to tighten it around the tail. "We got him!" he shouts as he runs from the small cave in order to get away from the excited crocodile. "Don't pull! Don't pull!" he repeats to the others who are holding the rope for him. "Take the pole!" he says and turns around to guide the croc out of the water. "Whew, man! He's coming after us," says Barr in surprise as the croc continues to move around quickly.

---

[11]**capture pole:** a long stick with a rope on the end used to capture animals

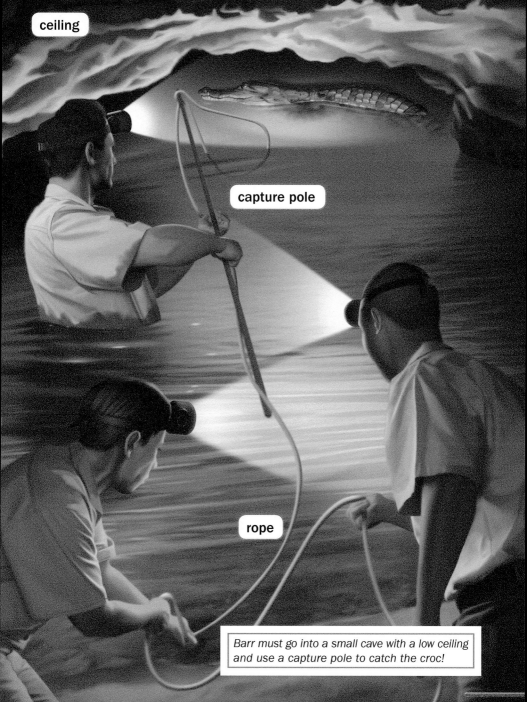

ceiling

capture pole

rope

Barr must go into a small cave with a low ceiling and use a capture pole to catch the croc!

Once the crocodile is under control, the team quickly tapes its dangerous mouth shut, examines the animal, and takes its measurements. "**I'll bet you**[12] this is two meters!" says Barr, "I'll bet you this is a six-foot croc!" A crocodile that size can be a dangerous animal and this fact is not missed by Barr. "Did you see me disappear in there?" he asks the team as they work, "I was scared. I mean, it got deeper and deeper and the ceiling was coming down … " It seems that even an experienced scientist like Dr. Brady Barr still respects how dangerous crocodiles can be!

The risk, though, is well worth the effort. After all, the result will be an important contribution to science. Dr. Barr and his team will be the first scientists ever to collect tissue samples from crocodiles deep in a cave. As they take these samples, they evaluate the health of the croc, "Look at that! Very healthy," says Barr as he looks closely at the animal. "We'll get a tissue sample," he says and then explains, "We'll take that tissue sample to a geneticist and they can hopefully solve some of the **riddles**[13] surrounding these Nile crocodiles in Madagascar."

At last the testing is done and they're ready to release the animal. "All right," says Barr as he stands up, "Let's let this guy go." As Barr holds the croc's mouth shut, he asks the guide to release the animal's tail. "Okay, let go. You ready?" he asks, and then releases the animal's mouth and steps back. The croc moves quickly towards the water and swims away unhurt.

---

[12]**I'll bet you:** *(slang)* an expression used to indicate that one is sure something is true
[13]**riddle:** a mystery

The team gathers their equipment and heads back towards the mouth of the cave. It's been a long day. To learn more about these reptiles, the scientists will need a lot more information. But for the moment, they feel that they've gotten enough to start their research.

At this point, the team must go their separate ways. Dr. Barr will go back to the U.S. to work on another project, and Garcia will stay in Madagascar to continue working with these mysterious crocodiles. The team may not have caught the enormous croc that they suspect is in the caves, but the expedition was still a great success. Hopefully, one day they will be able to return to continue their search for the giant cave crocs!

Summarize

Imagine that you are a member of the expedition team. Tell or write the story of this visit to the caves. Include the following information:

1. Where did you go and how did you get there?

2. What was it like in the caves?

3. What was it like when you captured the large crocodile?

4. Would you do it again? Why or why not?

After You Read

1. Crocodiles are called 'living dinosaurs' because:
 A. They live in Madagascar.
 B. They are amphibious.
 C. They are reptiles who live in caves.
 D. They have lived on Earth a long time.

2. Who does 'he's' refer to in paragraph 1 on page 6?
 A. a man from Spain
 B. a herpetologist
 C. a poacher
 D. a biologist

3. Which of the following is NOT a good heading for page 9?
 A. Noisy Scientists Take Boat Trip
 B. Team Arrives at Crocodile Cave
 C. Map Shows Hard Journey Ahead
 D. Local Guide Assists Group

4. What is the main purpose of paragraph 2 on page 10?
 A. to show that the journey is dangerous
 B. to introduce doubt about the expedition
 C. to explain the goals of the expedition
 D. to point out that the team is not paying attention

5. The footprints that Dr. Barr finds are _____ fresh.
 A. even
 B. still
 C. hardly
 D. much

6. What is Dr. Barr's attitude towards the footprints?
 A. amazed
 B. uncertain
 C. nervous
 D. doubting

7. The first crocodile that the team finds is:
    A. enormous
    B. unafraid
    C. shiny
    D. small

8. What happens when the young crocodile gets scared?
    A. It calls another crocodile.
    B. It bites the scientist.
    C. It escapes from the team.
    D. It uses its sense organ.

9. The word 'pleasant' in paragraph 1 on page 22 can be replaced by:
    A. kind
    B. gentle
    C. amusing
    D. heartfelt

10. How does the team use the capture pole to get a crocodile?
    A. They put the pole in dark water.
    B. They take tissue samples with the pole.
    C. They tighten the pole around the tail.
    D. They find an eye shine with the pole.

11. Which of the following is a good headline for page 25?
    A. Famous Doctor Hates Dangerous Crocs
    B. Scientist Describes Frightening Capture
    C. Risky Expedition Not Successful
    D. Team Refuses to Release Animal

12. What does the writer probably think about this research trip?
    A. The scientists work better separately.
    B. The huge crocodile does not exist.
    C. The expedition is a good beginning.
    D. The team should return home as soon as possible.

Nature's Survivor:
THE CROCODILE

Crocodiles are among the oldest species of animals on the face of the earth. At one time they shared the same environment as the dinosaurs, however the dinosaurs disappeared about 65 million years ago. Today, crocodile populations are growing in many places and several types of crocodile are no longer endangered. There are currently 23 different species from the crocodile family in 90 countries and islands around the world.

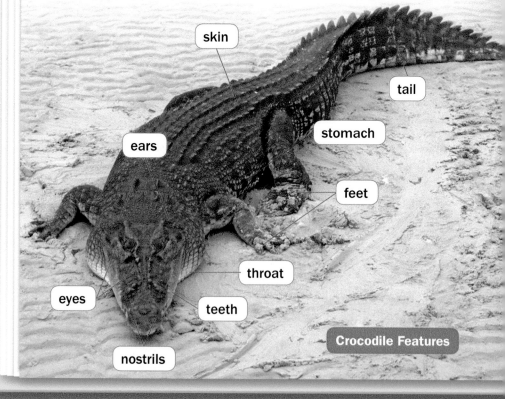

skin

tail

ears

stomach

feet

eyes

throat

teeth

nostrils

Crocodile Features

Special Teeth: The crocodile's teeth are well-designed to grip and hold things.

Nostrils on the Top: The crocodile's nostrils are on the top, not the front, of its head. This allows the animal to breathe while almost completely hidden under the water.

Functional Skin: The croc's skin is very thick and strong, which provides protection if it is attacked by a natural enemy. Its skin color also helps it disappear in its environment. This helps a croc when it is hunting and does not want to be seen.

A Strong Tail: The crocodile's tail allows it to change direction very quickly which helps it catch escaping animals when hunting.

Why has the crocodile survived for so long?

The crocodile is a true survivor. Firstly, unlike the dinosaur, the crocodile has been able to change physically, or adapt, as the earth's climate has changed over the past 200 million years. Secondly, crocodiles are unusually good at getting over diseases and injuries of many kinds. Illnesses that affect other animals in the same environment do not seem to affect the crocodiles. A croc can also be seriously injured, perhaps losing a leg or tail in a fight, and still survive for many years. A third reason that crocodiles have survived for so long is that they can eat almost anything—plant or animal. If the environment changes or they are forced to move to a new area, they can eat whatever is available. They are also able to go for very long periods of time—up to a year— without eating. Finally, crocodiles produce a lot of young. A mother croc usually lays as many as 30 eggs at a time, and it is not unusual for 80 to 90 percent of them to hatch.

CD 1, Track 04

Word Count: 362
Time: _____

Vocabulary List

amphibious (2, 4)
aptly (9)
bare (19)
capture (3, 6, 19, 22, 27)
capture pole (22, 23)
cave (2, 3, 4, 6, 9, 10, 13, 14, 16, 19, 20, 22, 23, 25, 26, 27)
cliff (9)
dinosaur (3, 4)
distress (20)
enormous (14, 19, 26)
expedition (3, 6, 9, 10, 26, 27)
flashlight (10, 13, 16)
geneticist (3, 20, 25)
herpetologist (2, 6)
I'll bet you (25)
nest (20)
passageway (13)
poacher (6)
reptile (2, 4, 26)
riddle (25)
species (2, 6)
tissue sample (3, 20, 22, 25)

Metric Conversion Chart

Area
1 hectare = 2.471 acres

Length
1 centimeter = .394 inches
1 meter = 1.094 yards
1 kilometer = .621 miles

Temperature
0° Celsius = 32° Fahrenheit

Volume
1 liter = 1.057 quarts

Weight
1 gram = .035 ounces
1 kilogram = 2.2 pounds